table for one

one

nekorn lammayot

D1563999

to my precious sons,
you are my heart, mind and soul

to my sister dao,
you punk!

to the brightest star i know,
because of you
i put down words
here and there
now and then

contents

table for one

every time i look
into her deep brown eyes
even for a moment
all i can see
is her close to me
sailing the deep blue seas
her mind so open and free
laying on pure white sands
her feminine body calls to me
with each caress of my hands
her beauty glows evermore
with each kiss under the full moon
with each long embrace at sunset
her heart and soul sings to me
why has it taken so many years?
i can't believe through my tired eyes
what i see in her deep brown eyes

-deep brown eyes

table for one

so beautiful
your long, ebony hair
glistening in the sun
so beautiful
your deep brown eyes
warm and inviting
like long summer nights
so beautiful
your cute, lovely nose
pointing to the stars
so beautiful
your natural, full lips
shimmering in the moonlight
so eternally beautiful
all of your face
like nature's great landscape

    -nature's great landscape

table for one

she's average, or so she says
but how can that be when i see
a face lovely as can be
she's normal, or so she says
but how can that be when i hear
a voice sweet as can be
she's plain, or so she says
but how can that be when i feel
a life vibrant as can be
she's regular, or so she says
but how can that be when i smell
sweet fragrances as she passes me
she's dull, or so she says
but how can that be when i feel
her spirit free as can be
she's ordinary, or so she says
but how can that be when my love
runs deep as the sea

-an ordinary girl

table for one

cozy, comfy space
in bright, summer colors
with its perfect views
and sounds that soothe
the view of the sea
the sounds of the sea
the tastes of the sea
wash and drown
all the greys
in my head

    -home by the sea

table for one

there are hearts of hearts
and souls of souls
walking on mother earth
who have come and gone
but no one i know
of flesh and bones
you are my first
chi trang

-chi trang

table for one

dia·na
when you walk my way
it sure makes my day

dia·na
so nice to see
your lovely face
and simple grace
those brown eyes
and warm smiles

dia·na
how are you?
how's your day?
i'd love to hear
what you have to say

dia·na
to say your name
a simple pleasure
that can't be measured

dia·na
you make me tremble
make me shy
still, through my days
i stop and wonder
if you'll head my way

-dia·na

table for one

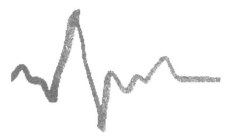

unsupported
suspended here
in emptiness
you can hear
the faint murmur
of being broken
as you lie
choking and gasping
you can feel
that faint murmur
from being broken
flat line

-flat line

table for one

stuck in our ways
we lost mondays
random thoughts
northern lights
and yellow sparks
our playdates
and fuck days
cease to exist
every time we persist

    -differences

table for one

i've walked
through broken lines
and broken vows
i've felt
innocent cries
through guilty lies
i believed
in empty truths
that sets us free
i know
the causes and effects
of life's hardest tests
i've struggled
through endless, sleepless nights
in cold, empty spaces
i get it
the hard lines
on these faces

-hard lines

table for one

another year older
through all my patience
still part of life
she's mother to
my heart, mind, and soul
not a penny more
my precious sons
listen without prejudice
it's what we need more of
for all of us to grow
you see, it's faith
not blame and hate
as nothing was conspired
nor desired
then why all of this
to take another's bliss?
my precious sons
when endings come
life only knows
how one learns to grow

      -precious sons

table for one

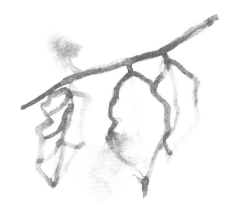

dry, dead leaves
from weathered, old trees
falls gently on my street
and a subtle, cool air
breezes through me
fall is here
its colors of art
against her greys
its cool comfort
where we used to play
it's something in the air
or how she prepares
her long, dark hair
i love her art
even as we part

on october fall
my love was born
i feel blessed
and i feel torn

      -october fall

table for one

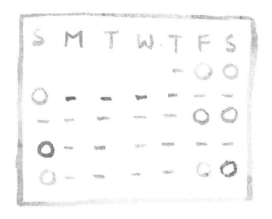

in this unhappy place
eating just to fill
but unfilled
you see
there's no taste
when you're stuck
in life's rut
consumed by random thoughts
wondering how and why
i made them cry
shedding all my tears
thinking of those years

-first, third, and fifth

table for one

i felt her from afar
was it her presence?
her youthful exuberance?
her porcelain light
or simple grace?
no matter
it's too late
she's in my landscape, now
time can't erase
my image of
her cute, lovely face

-kristee

table for one

you're the one
the only one
you got this
let go of your shit
and get through it
be small
be true
to be free
from what the mind sees
share your breath
with mother earth
know your death
and life's simple pleasures
it's always been
you, you, and you
so dream out loud
and live right now
this, i believe
is what we need

-true

table for one

i don't see all the colors
don't even hear all there is
but i see something special in thee
and i'd know just how to listen
why is that, you ask?
cause i get it
the stars, moon, and trees
i feel their beauty
what it means to be free
and how it's all connected
to the deepest part of thee

                    -thee

table for one

my dear
another year wasted
and i don't know
how we came to this
still, i love you
and we'd be kissing
if it wasn't for all of that
how i've missed you
wishing you wouldn't do just that
and as each year passes
my fear starts to fade
but look at the mess we made

-distant

table for one

you've cold feet?
is it too soon?
well, hear all of me
it's neither impatience
nor recklessness
it's my excitement
commitment
it's my desire
to call thee darling
that sweet, endearing sound
with no bound
to say darling
lose your fear
and be my dear

-darling

table for one

you're lovely
hope you know
working your way
to make their day
your lovely tattoos
you being you
strength, baby, strength
and your smile
makes us stay awhile
bartender girl
you're so much more
making that difference
in our world

    -bartender girl

table for one

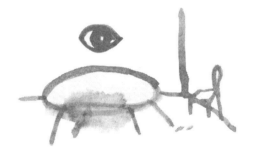

table for one
i'll tip well
when i'm done
cause it's awkward
with no one
its painful comfort
across all that's complete
i look up to count
two, four...,six
feels like defeat
seven, eight...,nine
hurry up and dine

     -table for one

table for one

my boys
they're beautiful
not one
but two
how can one be
so lucky
to be blessed with
two
creative
lovely
thoughtful
boys
they're
twice my joy

-two

table for one

when the evening storms passes
the morning turns crisp and clear
yet my mind is a mess
from last night
thoughts of gratitude
and all this need to feel blessed
neither calm nor soothe
once bold and brave
now, just a hollow human cave

-hollow

table for one

to whom do you give
your flat, bright screens
your wishes and dreams
your beliefs and
disbeliefs?
your day fantasies
your second pal
or gal?
away from home
and on your phone
to whom do you give?
stop
listen
silence
to whom do we give?

                    -the giver

table for one

it's beautiful
exuberant
i'm feeling full and light
by these colors and lights
of wonder days and nights
yearning no more
being true and free

in the beauty of now
i'm breathing in life
without strife

-dalabua

table for one

friends come
friends go
only one life
baby, shine bright
cause there is no other
love comes
love goes
only tonight
baby, live life
cause there is no other
she'll get you
what you want
what you need
from this life
baby, she'll fight
cause there is no other
mother in this world

       -mother

table for one

gentle, supple ripples
in perfect centric motions
fills this man-made
narrow body of water
humdrum sounds
from spinning wheels
designed by man
burning endless miles
over weather-worn concrete
laid down by men
drifting
drifting
drifting away
in useless, random thoughts
of all the things we fought
all man-made

-man-made

table for one

she doesn't want to be with me
but it's okay
i've got me
he doesn't want to be with you
but it's okay
you've got you
she doesn't care to comfort me
but it's alright
i've got me
he doesn't care to comfort you
but it's alright
you've got you
she doesn't love this part of me
but it's okay
i'll love all of me
he doesn't love that part of you
but it's okay
you'll learn to love all of you

-borpenyang (no worries)

table for one

your lovely face
now, i know
there's no turning back
from your everglow
it's heaven-sent
to my heart
your lovely face
like nature's art

i'm amazed and smitten
hopin' and wishin'
our time will start

-nhi

table for one

when nina sings karaoke
her voice is so clear
it makes me long to be near
and her highs and cries
takes me high as the sky
when nina sings karaoke
it's neat
better than okay
it's saved
replayed and on repeat
cause it's so sweet

      -karaokay

table for one

my happy song
my happy beat
keeps moving my feet
where have you been?
cause i haven't seen
i needed you
been down so long
then you came along
my happy song
of bliss and joy
cause of my happy beat
i'm no longer in defeat
cause of my happy song
i'll keep humming along

-my happy song

table for one

i've been bad
with all i've had
now, empty and alone
through my bones
with my one regret
beating down my chest

-regret

table for one

mister ethan boy
and his toy
his colored rubik's
deck of cards
and polished violin
you see
to see his tricks
and hear his tunes
it's such a treat
and so, so sweet
yeah, my lovely son
the youngest one
is so much fun

    -mister ethan

table for one

you made me smile
so we chatted awhile
and shared our past
but nothing ever lasts
and nothing really changed
you see
your days must be blissful
your loving
and your life exuberant
this is me
sending best wishes
to all my misses

-my misses

table for one

going back in time
not to drag out the past
but to cherish
what we had
the dreams we shared
our despairs
and precious moments
just can't compare
but like incoming waves
in a sea of endless stars
our dreams washed away
along with the pure, white sands

-dreams

table for one

it hurts
as much as yesterday
someone, somewhere
show me the way
somewhere, somehow
show me how to play

-play

table for one

you've owned my heart
but like so many stars
that crashed and fell
the simple joys of life
from the warmth of your smile
your vibrant charm
remains hidden in my heart

-owner of a lonely heart

table for one

the brightest star i know
blinded me
bonded me
from and to
my worst fears
from and to
my happiest
and saddest tears
you, the brightest star i know
brought me to my knees
so i can see me

   -the brightest star i know

table for one

it's so sad, baby
suicidal sad
with only thoughts
from yesteryear
i'm so sad, baby
depression kind of sad
all alone
stuck in our past
i've grown suicidal sad

you must be glad
we didn't last

-suicidal sad

table for one

we run
round and round
chasing tons
wasting time
with our crime
we run
round and round
filling space
saving face
and losing grace
we run
round and round
from our fun
chasing none
till we're done

-run

table for one

goodbye, my darling
it's been a hell of a ride
you broke my pride
and made me cry
goodbye, my darling
it was incredible..., amazing
you've owned my heart
then tore me apart

-torn

table for one

she knew i was depressed
she knew i was sad
but all i ever did
was make her mad

-insensitive

table for one

not obsessed
not possessed
love is love
dove is dove
love is love
not above
not in fear
not in tears
love is love
not above
do you hear?
can you feel?
love is here

-l-o-v-e

table for one

@3 a.m.
i was wrong
i was sorry
i wasn't strong
i lost my ways
wasting precious days
i wish to be forgiven
@3a.m.
so early
yet so late
and no disrespect
just things i needed to clear
like useless thoughts and fears
stealing our years
forgive me
marry me?
be my wife
i promise a good life
cause you're in my very being
cause i love you
even as you're leaving
baby, marry me?
cause i no longer
want to suppress
and certainly don't want to regret

-@3a.m.

table for one

my son,
wherever
however
you are
whatever
you are doing
your father's love
will always be
for infinite
unconditional
indefinite

-alexander

table for one

let's explore k-culture
in vibrant sights and sounds
it's pure exuberance
through the colors of the seasons
their brilliant lives
like a secret garden
its crash-landings
and new beginnings
from beauties
with such graces
descendants of the sun
it's so much fun
and just to start
it's song hye kyo
lee minho
hyun bin
son ye jin
chae jung-an
and ha ji won
through their part
it'll touch your heart

      -secret garden

table for one

clear
concise
corporate
words
mask those who
rarely gets heard

      -cascade

table for one

NETFLIX

too comfortable
too anxious
waiting
waiting
waiting
going solo
freedom galore
yet nothing to explore
with the enemy of the best
putting me to the test
shall i unhinge?
continue to binge?

just wasting time
on my dime

-creature comfort

table for one

we're fine
drinking wine
yet borderline
so why not break free?
and be joy
like that girl and boy

    -it's gonna be fun!

table for one

deep, painful
emotional, physical impressions
memories of body and mind
are all that's left
and you've barely slept

so nothing more to say or do
we really are through
and all that remains
is not the same
seems like nothing ever lasts
except our broken past

-memories

table for one

change
it's coming
ready or not
connecting your dots
change
it's here
then disappears
kicking your rear
change
good or bad
maybe you never had
change
it's you
it's me
just the way
it's got to be

-change

table for one

i'm no good
just a thief of hearts
breaking families
and tearing myself apart
i'm no good
isolated by guilt
maybe that's how i'm built
i lost it all
yet nothing seems to break this fall
perhaps, i'm no good
or just misunderstood
ignorance was bliss
now, i know
when i'm dead and gone
i'm not one
who'll be missed

-thief of hearts

table for one

it's cold tonight
let's make ramen
in a pot
while it's hot
add an egg
some kimchi
and when it's done
click season one

-season one

table for one

harsh words
can hurt
but you, my dear
shining so brightly and all
you text it loud and proud
with all your exclamations

-exclamations

table for one

flustered
tangled emotions
lives twisting in motion
betrayal of devotion
what seemed so right
so sudden, so fast
didn't even last
immature
hadn't loved
haven't grown
hadn't known
how to handle
how to love
a love
like hers

-hers

table for one

never again
will i be
lonely
nor clingy
to anyone
or anything

deleting all
my random thoughts
in the dark
never again
will they spark

      -never

table for one

i will conquer alone
to be my own

    -one and only

table for one

life isn't meant to be easy
it's to be experienced
so don't hold back
be brave
i told myself
but tomorrow never came

-tick-tock

table for one

love comes calling
are you ready?
its elusive nature
its pure bliss and joy
love comes calling
to knock you down
strip you of things
that are no longer yours
no longer you
love comes calling
it's loud and clear
you're losing fear
oh dear
love comes calling
then fades
breaking you apart
tearing your heart
love comes calling
are you ready?
it's profound
it's begging, screaming, and crying
until there's no "i"
and no why

       -no why

table for one

no scene as vivid
as imaginative
nothing as deep
only in your head
can poems be read
in mystic delight
on your night

poetry
can be simple and profound
with no bound
to be said
all in your head

-poetry

table for one

it's hard to detach
from the past
even in sleep
i feel you deep
no, love doesn't hold
as stories unfold
and time isn't kind
to the heart and mind
falling into an abyss
smiling but crying
laughing yet dying
in the end
it's definite
infinite
you're a part of me
through and through
what to do

-impressions

table for one

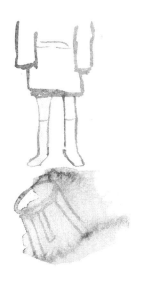

i'm ready
gearing up
with stuff in my head
seeing how i'll be dead
and how they'll shed
no longer empty in my bed
no worries
no sorrows
no tomorrows
cause today, i'm ready
playing it all in my head
how and when i'll be dead

since it's all in my head
better close my eyes instead

-ready

table for one

suppressed
no one cares
you see
it's toxic
selfish
unstable
unworthy
repulsive
cause i'm dead weight
pulling them down
with my frown

-frown

table for one

come sit with me
there's nothing here
only newfound silence
breathing in
listening in
to the life around
with eyes closed
our heavy thoughts
becomes floating clouds
just passing by

    -floating clouds

table for one

empty inside
i run and hide
asking myself
who are you
where are you
what are you
like a zombie
out of touch
in the mind
i'm living my crime
and in the depths of despair
i'm going nowhere

-zombie

table for one

unnoticed
uncounted
nowhere to be found
in this empty, christmas town
you see
when consciousness fades
we become
invisible
divisible
from all that's man-made
so wake up
time to realize
all is alive
living
breathing
this air
that we share

-20/20

table for one

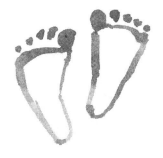

i chose this life
had i known
it would cut like a knife

-choose life

table for one

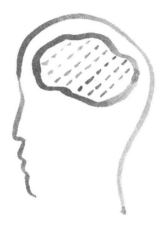

your mind
wants to bend something
into something it's not
so stop your plot

       -stories

table for one

this past week
it's been icy cold
frozen, broken pipes
and roads covered in ice
without water and light
nothing but darkness tonight
no family, friends, or neighbors
still, nothing to fear
no need to fret
like mother nature
we can adapt
we can exist
unless we resist

-black ice

table for one

i wasn't sure you'd stay
so i lost my will to play
i wasn't sure you'd feel
so i didn't feel like giving
i wasn't sure you knew
so i didn't let you be
i wasn't sure if you'd understand
so i couldn't stop
i wasn't sure of myself
and i didn't know my worth

i wasn't sure
so i couldn't
i didn't

        -certainty

table for one

they lived a full life
have you?

-hmmmmm

table for one

i dreamt of someone i shouldn't have
we were warm and cozy under the blanket
i've always admired her stillness
with her head now resting on my shoulders
i planted sweet kisses on her face
but my hands wouldn't stay still
they made their way to her...
then she nonchalantly said
my husband is over there
relieved
i slowly opened my eyes
and let out a long, silent sigh

-fantasy

table for one

i've observed
how others lived
in their homes
it's genuine and warm
chaotic at times
but their own
you see
i'm a nomad
never my own
never my home
always alone
then i heard
a nomad
means one
who is not mad

-no mad

table for one

when i asked where you were
as i felt alone in a broken home
my karma
when i thought you'd come home
from the early wee hours
it wasn't an option
my karma
when i begged and pleaded
and my fear screamed out its lungs
wishing you hadn't heard
my karma
when i couldn't bring myself
to pop the question
my karma
my doing is my making
my karma

-karma

table for one

i love you
i love you
i love you
twenty-four seven
just like heaven

-what is love?

table for one

tonight, i feel so good
in my happy mood
holding your hands
and making plans
tonight, i feel so good
holding you tight
it just feels right
tonight, i feel so good
with my arms
around your hips
can't stop kissing your lips
tonight, it feels so good
cause we're understood

-my a.m.

table for one

i put down words
here and there
now and then
it's nourishment

-nourishment

table for one

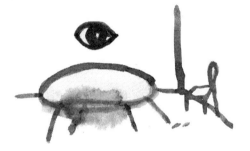

Made in the USA
Middletown, DE
18 March 2022